THE
FINANCIAL
PLANNING
WORKBOOK

Library of Congress Cataloging in Publication Data

Burkett, Larry.
  The financial planning workbook.

  1. Finance, Personal. 2. Budgets, Personal.
3. Finance, Personal—Religious aspects—
Christianity. I. Title.
HG179.B835 1982   332.024   82-7877
ISBN 0-8024-2546-1   AACR2

18 19 20 Printing/ML/Year 93 92 91 90 89 88

Printed in the United States of America

CONTENTS

INTRODUCTION

To many people, the word *budgeting* has a bad ring. Why? Because they see budgeting as a punishment plan. Unfortunately, this has often been the case with many families attempting to correct in one day financial problems that have been developing for several years.

It does not have to be so; a budget is simply a financial plan for the home. What is proposed in this workbook is a simple, workable plan for home money management; one that brings the financial area under God's control and relieves the burdens of worry, frustration, and anxiety. It maximizes family finances so that we are more effective for God both spiritually and financially. From this foundation the budget becomes a tool for good communications in an area normally characterized by conflict.

This workbook has been thoroughly tested as a tool to help families manage their finances. It is used in family workshop seminars taught by Christian Financial Concepts, Inc. Cassette tapes and instructor manuals are available for those who would like to teach this material in their communities. For further information contact: Christian Financial Concepts, Route 4 Hidden Lake, Dahlonega, Georgia 30533.

We are grateful to Mrs. Diana Helms for her efforts in developing this workbook.

SECTION *1*
Getting Started

GETTING STARTED

THE GOAL—LIVING WITHIN OUR MEANS

WHAT DOES THIS MEAN?

It means to spend no more than we make on a monthly basis. Ideally that means to live on a cash basis and not use credit or borrowed money to provide normal living expenses. It also means the self-discipline to control spending and keep needs, wants, and desires in their proper relationship.

Needs

These are the purchases necessary to provide your basic requirements such as food, clothing, home, medical coverage and others (1 Timothy 6:8).

WANTS

Wants involve choices about the quality of goods to be used. Dress clothes vs. work clothes, steak vs. hamburger, a new car vs. a used car, etc. 1 Peter 3:3-4 gives a point of reference for determining wants in a Christian's life.

DESIRES

These are choices according to God's plan that can be made only out of surplus funds after all other obligations have been met (1 John 2:15-16).

OBSTACLES TO GOOD PLANNING

Social pressures to own more "things."

The attitude that *more is better* regardless of the cost.

The use of credit to delay necessary decisions.

No surplus available to cope with rising prices and unexpected expenses.

We tend to offset increases in income by increasing our level of spending. That spending attitude is a real problem because it leads to:

THE DANGER POINT

When income barely equals outgo.

Break-even is not a *living point* but a *decision point*. If all the income is consumed in monthly expenses and something unusual happens, such as the family automobile breaking down, the result is additional indebtedness.

A decision is necessary at this point: *MAKE MORE MONEY OR SPEND LESS.*

Ideally this decision would be made before external pressures left few alternatives. Unfortunately when the pressure comes on, the credit card comes out. The result is a debt that cannot be paid. That limits the alternatives to treating the "symptoms." Some typical treatments are: bill consolidation loans, additional credit, second mortgages, or a job for the wife. Those may provide temporary relief. But, unfortunately, since only the symptom has been treated the problem still exists. It's only a matter of time until the symptoms reappear.

It is obviously better to cut expenses than to attempt to increase income. Unfortunately, it is also painful. The key? *Commitment.*

RECOGNIZE THE DIVISIONS OF INCOME
(figure 1.1)

The *first* part belongs to God. It is returned to Him as a tithe in recognition that He owns all that we have. We are merely stewards.

> Will a man rob God? Yet you are robbing me! But you say, "How have we robbed Thee?" In tithes and contributions.
> Malachi 3:8

The *government* wants its share.

> Then He said to them, "Then render to Caesar the things that are Caesar's and to God the things that are God's."
> Matthew 22:21

Family needs come next.

> But if anyone does not provide for his own, and especially for those of his household, he has denied the faith, and is worse than an unbeliever.
> 1 Timothy 5:8

The portion available after tithe and taxes is termed *net spendable income.*

God says pay your *debts.*

> The wicked borrows and does not pay back, but the righteous is gracious and gives.
> Psalm 37:21

Faithful management will yield a fifth portion.

The creation of a *surplus* should be a major goal for the Christian. It is the surplus that allows us to respond to the needs of others.

> At this present time your abundance being a supply for their want, that their abundance also may become a supply for our want, that there may be equality.
> 2 Corinthians 8:14

Even if a family is not in debt, their finances should be budget controlled to maximize the surplus.

7

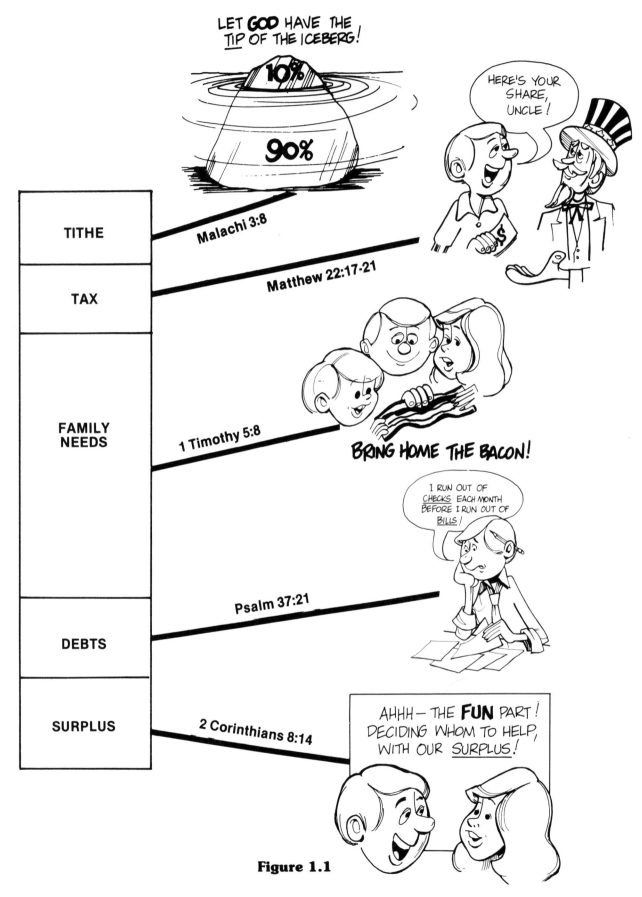

Figure 1.1

In addition to responding to needs of others, it's the surplus that provides the flexibility to meet emergencies without credit. That surplus can also be used to invest and multiply your assets.

WHERE DO WE START?

Starting a budget is just like starting on a trip. You cannot set a course without first determining where you are.

Step one: The budget: What is the present level of spending?

Step two: Budget goals: Establish the "ideal" budget. In actuality, few people ever reach the ideal. But it is possible to establish the "now" condition by reviewing the ideal.

In establishing a budget this trip will consist of comparing the present spending level with a guideline for balanced spending. The comparison will point out where adjustments should be made.

Once the budget is established, the control system must be incorporated that will keep spending on the "road." The system must be able to sound the alarm *before* overspending occurs.

THERE ARE ROAD HAZARDS

DISCOURAGEMENT:

To complete the trip one must keep going. A major problem is to develop a budget and then *not* follow it.

LEGALISM:

Another problem is becoming legalistic and inflexible. Then the budget becomes a family weapon instead of a family tool. Becoming legalistic incidentally seems to occur at the same time the money runs out. If a road is blocked we usually have to take another route to get where we are going. Remain flexible to necessary changes.

OVERCORRECTION:

When the money gets tight, the tendency is to eliminate clothes, entertainment, food, and other "expendables." That creates a pressure that is often relieved by overspending in other areas.

EVERYBODY NEEDS A BUDGET!

Financial bondage can result from a lack of money and overspending. But it can also be caused from the misuse of an abundance of money. Some families have enough money to be undisciplined and get away with it (financially speaking). But true financial freedom requires that we be good stewards (Matthew 24:45). That is only possible with self-discipline.

A good plan requires *action* and *discipline* to make it work.

It may require sacrifice.

Begin *now!*

SECTION 2
Where Are We?

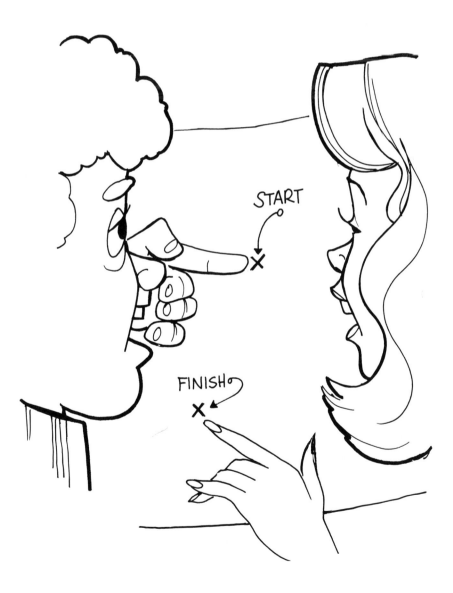

DETERMINING MONTHLY INCOME
AND EXPENSES

THE PRESENT CONDITION

On the monthly Income and Expenses form (figure 2.1) compare actual monthly expenses with monthly income to determine present spending. (Note: You may need to keep a diary of expenses for a few months before you can accurately determine actual monthly expenses.)

To determine living cost, consider what represents a reasonable standard of living at your present income level. Reasonable, *not total,* sacrifices are necessary.

Therefore, when you set up your budget, include a reasonable amount for personal spending, e.g., clothes, savings, entertainment, recreation.

DETERMINING INCOME PER MONTH

NOTE: Use form 1 (Monthly Income and Expenses Sheet) for this section.

List all gross income (income before deductions) in the "Income Per Month" section on the Monthly Income and Expenses Sheet. Don't forget to consider commissions, bonuses, fees, tips, periodic savings withdrawals, allowances, gifts, loans.

When income consists totally or partially of commissions or other fluctuating sources, average it for a year and divide by twelve. Use a low yearly average, not a high average.

If you are paid on a weekly or bi-weekly basis, take the total yearly income and divide by twelve.

Business expense reimbursements should not be considered family income. Avoid the trap of using expense money to buffer family spending or the result will be an indebtedness that cannot be paid.

WHAT IS "NET SPENDABLE INCOME"?

Net spendable income is that portion available for family spending. Some of your income does not belong to the family and therefore cannot be spent. For instance:

THE TITHE: Ten percent of your total income belongs to God. For a detailed discussion on the tithe, see *Your Finances in Changing Times* by Larry Burkett, published by Moody Press; chapter 10, "Sharing—God's Way."

TAXES: Federal withholding, social security, and state and local taxes must also be deducted from gross income. Self-employed individuals must not forget to set aside money for quarterly payments on taxes. Beware of the tendency to treat unpaid tax money as windfall profit.

OTHER DEDUCTIONS: Payroll deductions for insurance, credit union savings or debt payments, bonds, stock programs, retirement, and union dues can be handled in either of two ways:

1. Treat them as a deduction from gross income the same as the income taxes.
2. Include them in spendable income and deduct them from the proper category. This is preferred because it provides a more accurate picture of where the money is being spent.

EXAMPLE: A deduction is being made for credit union savings. This amount should be considered as a part of income with an expense shown under "Savings" for the same amount. This method makes it easier to see the overall effect the deduction has on the family budget.

NET SPENDABLE INCOME = GROSS INCOME MINUS TITHE AND MINUS TAXES.

HOW IS NET SPENDABLE INCOME BEING SPENT?

HOUSING EXPENSES: All monthly expenses necessary to operate the home, including taxes, insurance, maintenance, and utilities. The amount used for utility payments should be an average monthly amount for the past twelve months.

If you cannot establish an accurate maintenance expense, use 10 percent of the monthly mortgage payment.

FOOD EXPENSES: All grocery expenses, including paper goods and non-food products normally purchased at grocery stores. Include milk, bread, and items purchased in addition to regular shopping trips. *Do not include* eating out and daily lunches eaten away from home.

If you do not know your actual food expenses, keep a detailed spending record for thirty to forty-five days.

AUTOMOBILE EXPENSES: Includes payments, insurance, gas, oil, maintenance, depreciation, etc.

Depreciation is actually the money set aside to repair or replace the automobile. The minimum amount set aside should be sufficient to keep the car in decent repair and to replace it at least every four to five years.

If replacement funds are not available in the budget, the minimum allocation should be maintenance costs. Annual or semi-annual auto insurance payments should be set aside on a monthly basis, thereby avoiding the crisis of a neglected expense.

INSURANCE: Includes all insurance, such as health, life, disability, not associated with the home or auto.

DEBTS: Includes all monthly payments required to meet debt obligations. Home mortgage and automobile payments are not included here.

ENTERTAINMENT AND RECREATION: Vacation savings, camping trips, club dues, sporting equipment, hobby expenses, and athletic events. Don't forget little league expense, booster clubs, and so on.

The only effective method of budgeting for entertainment and recreation is to decide on a reasonable allocation and stick with it.

CLOTHING: The average annual amount spent on clothes divided by twelve. The minimum amount should be at least ten dollars per month per family member.

SAVINGS: Every family should allocate something for savings. A savings account can provide funds for emergencies and is a key element in good planning and financial freedom.

MEDICAL EXPENSES: Insurance deductibles, doctors' bills, eye glasses, drugs, orthodontist visits, etc. Use a yearly average divided by twelve to determine a monthly amount.

MISCELLANEOUS: Unusual expenses that do not seem to fit anywhere else; nursery expenses for working mothers, special or private education costs, pocket allowance (coffee money), miscellaneous gifts, Christmas presents, etc.

Miscellaneous spending is usually underestimated. A thirty to forty-five day spending record is usually necessary to establish accurate present spending habits. Self-discipline is the key to controlling miscellaneous spending.

INCOME VS. EXPENSES

STEP ONE: Compile the expenses under each of the major categories (items 3 through 12) and note this as the total expense. Then in the space provided, subtract expenses from net spendable income.

STEP TWO: *If income is greater than expenses,* you need only to control spending to maximize the surplus. Section 5 will help you to do this.

STEP THREE: *If expenses are greater than income,* a detailed analysis will be necessary to correct the situation and restore a proper balance. Proceed to the next section.

WHERE ARE YOU?

MONTHLY INCOME & EXPENSES

INCOME PER MONTH _____

Salary $1,250
Interest   _____
Dividends   _____
Notes   _____
Rents   _____

TOTAL GROSS INCOME   1,250

LESS:

1. Tithe   125

2. Tax   187

NET SPENDABLE INCOME   938

3. Housing   391
Mortgage (rent)   260
Insurance   _____
Taxes   _____
Electricity   52
Gas   28
Water   6
Sanitation   5
Telephone   20
Maintenance   20
Other   _____

4. Food   230

5. Automobile(s)   85
Payments   _____
Gas & Oil   40
Insurance   20
License   3
Taxes   4
Maint./Repair/ Replacement   18

6. Insurance   39
Life   29
Medical   10
Other   _____

7. Debts   90
Credit Card   80
Loans & Notes   10
Other   _____

8. Enter. & Recreation   53
Eating Out   20
Trips   _____
Babysitters   8
Activities   10
Vacation   _____
Other   15

9. Clothing   50

10. Savings   _____

11. Medical Expenses   30
Doctor   10
Dentist   15
Drugs   5
Other   _____

12. Miscellaneous   69
Toiletry, cosmetics   10
Beauty, barber   15
Laundry, cleaning   15
Allowances, lunches   16
Subscriptions   3
Gifts (incl. Christmas)   10
Special Education   _____
Cash   _____
Other   _____

TOTAL EXPENSES   1037

INCOME VS. EXPENSE
Net Spendable Income   938

Less Expenses   1037

   -99

Figure 2.1

SECTION 3

Short-Range Planning

17

HANDLING THE VARIABLES BY SHORT-RANGE PLANNING

WHAT IS SHORT-RANGE PLANNING?

Budgeting for irregular expenses on a monthly basis. That includes fluctuating utility bills, auto maintenance, medical expenses, clothing, etc.

EXAMPLE: 1. By averaging utility bills over one year, money can be stored from low use months to offset the cost of high use months.

2. Annual or semi-annual insurance payments are met by establishing a monthly reserve.

Expenditures for clothing, medical and dental bills are other examples for which provision should be made. Those items normally are not purchased on a regular basis. Without the needed reserves, the result is often additional debt when those purchases must be made.

A vacation can be planned the same way. Plan what is needed for the coming year's vacation and divide the amount by twelve to determine what must be saved on a monthly basis.

Items such as automobiles, appliances, and household goods (furniture, rugs, drapes, etc.) wear out or deteriorate over time. Periodic allocations should be made to replace those items as necessary.

Ideally, automobile depreciation and maintenance should be allocated on a monthly basis. That savings would then pay for maintenance, insurance, and replacement of the automobile (assuming the car is kept for five years or 100,000 miles).

A DANGER—the tendency in tight budgeting situations is to avoid maintenance and depreciation savings with the excuse that "we just can't afford it." Even if the full amount cannot be set aside, try to save something for those purposes. Depreciation is the same as any other expense. Without money to repair a car, the usual alternative is to replace it—on the time payment plan!

Failure to plan for short-range variables and depreciating items results in crisis planning. Control your expenditures; don't let them control you.

HOW TO DO THIS

Use the table illustrated in figure 3.2 to determine how much must be allocated to the various categories. For example, if automobile insurance is $120 per year, set aside $10 per month so that the bill can be paid when due.

Include those amounts in the proper categories when planning the total budget (use form 2).

At the end of each month the allocated money not actually used is transferred to a savings account. The savings ledger shows the various categories for which money is being saved (form 6).

ESTABLISH ACCOUNT LIMITS. Each account should have a predetermined limit. Once that limit has been reached, no additional savings are necessary.

18

EXAMPLE: Assume $360 is the yearly total for medical expenses. Once the savings for medical reaches $360, the needed reserve has been met. Unless greater medical expenses are expected, savings beyond $360 is not necessary. Monthly funds can then be applied elsewhere until a medical expense occurs that reduces the amount in savings.

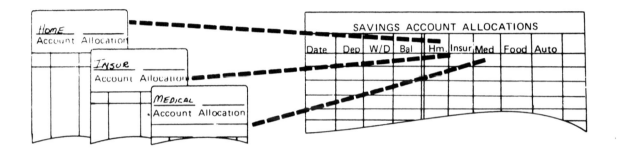

Figure 3.1

Remember, the plan is to establish a reserve for variables, depreciating items, maintenance, or special needs such as fluctuating income. The savings account ledger divides the surplus by budget category.

BE FLEXIBLE. In starting a budget, it may be necessary to borrow from one account to supplement another. For example, if the car breaks down before a surplus is accumulated in the auto account, it may be necessary to borrow from the clothing or medical surpluses to pay for the car repair. However, to continue to do that month after month will defeat the long-range purpose in budgeting.

That purpose is to *Plan ahead!*

	Estimated Cost	Per Month
1. VACATION	$_____ ÷12	$_____
2. DENTIST	$ _180_ ÷12	$ _15_
3. DOCTOR	$ _120_ ÷12	$ _10_
4. AUTOMOBILE	$ _204_ ÷12	$ _17_
5. ANNUAL INSURANCE	$_____ ÷12	$_____
(Life)	$_____ ÷12	$_____
(Health)	$_____ ÷12	$_____
(Auto)	$ _240_ ÷12	$ _20_
(Home)	$_____ ÷12	$_____
6. CLOTHING	$ _600_ ÷12	$ _50_
7. INVESTMENTS	$_____ ÷12	$_____
8. OTHER	$_____ ÷12	$_____

Figure 3.2

Budget Problems

BUDGET PROBLEM AREAS

BEWARE! Unforeseen problems can wreck your budget. Those include:

Bookkeeping Errors. . . . Impulse Buying. . . . Hidden Debts. . . . Gifts. . . .

BOOKKEEPING ERRORS

An accurately balanced checkbook is a must. Even small errors result in big problems if they are allowed to compound.

An inaccurate balance can result in an overdrawn account, as well as in significant bank charges.

Automatic banking systems create additional pitfalls. Automatic payment deductions must be subtracted from the checkbook ledger at the time they are paid by the bank.

> EXAMPLE: An insurance premium is paid by automatic withdrawal on the fifteenth of each month. Since no statement or notice is received from the insurance company, you must make certain that on the fifteenth of every month the proper amount is deducted from your home checking account records.
>
> The same situation would be true for automatic credit card payments or any other automatic withdrawal.

Direct deposits into checking accounts and automatic teller transactions must also be noted in the home ledger at the proper time. *Don't forget* to include bank service charges in the home ledger.

DANGER! Automatic overdraft protection (credit used to cover deficits) is really a device to avoid good bookkeeping and accumulate additional debts.

To balance your home checkbook ledger against the monthly bank statement properly, follow the steps illustrated in figure 4.1.

OTHER FACTORS IN KEEPING GOOD RECORDS:

1. *Use a ledger type checkbook rather than a stub type.* The ledger gives greater visibility and lends itself to fewer errors.

2. *Make certain all checks are accounted for.* All checks should be entered in the ledger when written. This entry must include the check number, amount, date, and assignee.

3. *One bookkeeper only.* When more than one individual attempts to maintain the record system, confusion usually results. If the system is in good order, either the husband or the wife can keep the records. The choice should be based on who can do the job best. If the records are in a mess, the husband should assume the responsibility for correcting the situation.

4. *Maintain a home ledger.* If all records are kept in a checkbook ledger, you run the risk of losing it. A home ledger eliminates this possibility and makes record keeping more orderly.

CHECKBOOK BALANCE PROCEDURE

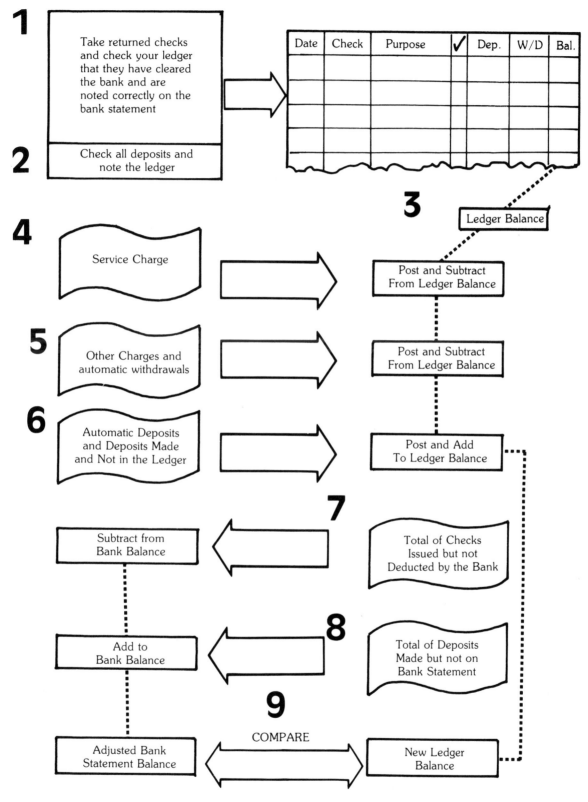

Figure 4.1

5. *Balance the account — every month — to the penny.* Never allow the home ledger and bank statement to disagree in balance. The two most common errors are arithmetic errors (addition or subtraction) and transposition errors (writing in the wrong amount). Use a calculator and balance the account *to the penny.*

HIDDEN DEBTS

A common error is to overlook non-monthly debts such as doctor bills, family loans, bank notes, etc. Thus, when payments come due, there is no budget allocation for them.

To avoid surprises, establish and maintain a list of debts in total. The list must be reviewed and revised on a periodic basis and the budget must anticipate necessary payments.

The list should reflect progress made on debt payments and can serve as a "payoff goal" sheet. Begin with a goal of eliminating the smallest debt first. Then double up on the next debt, and so on until all debts are eliminated.

A suggested form is shown in Figure 5. Note that space is provided for the name and number of the person to contact in the event of a problem.

IMPULSE BUYING

Impulse items are unnecessary purchases made on the spur-of-the-moment.

These purchases are usually rationalized by, "It was on sale," "I was planning to buy it anyway," "I've always wanted one," "I just couldn't resist it," or "I owe it to myself." Often they are made with a credit card because the cash isn't available. The net result is a little-used item and an unnecessary debt.

"Impulse purchases" are not restricted to small items. They range from homes, cars, and trips to unscheduled luncheons. Cost is not the issue; necessity is. Every purchase should be considered in light of the budget.

Discipline is the key to controlling "impulse" buying. If necessary, resort to the self-imposed discipline of the "impulse" buying sheet shown in figure 4.2.

Establish the discipline that before buying on impulse, you will list the item on the impulse sheet, along with the date and the cost. Furthermore, wait thirty days before purchasing the item and during that time get at least two additional prices.

If you feel you still need the item at the end of the thirty days and the money is available, then buy it. You will eliminate most impulse items by this discipline.

GIFTS

A major budget-buster in most families is overspending on gifts. Tradition dictates a gift for nearly every occasion. Unfortunately, the net result is often a gift someone else doesn't want, purchased with money that was needed for something else.

Many times the cost is increased because the gift is selected at the last moment. If gifts are a part of normal spending, budget for them and buy ahead—reasonably.

To bring the cost of gifts under control, consider doing the following:

1. Keep an event calendar for the year and budget ahead.
2. Determine not to buy any gifts on credit (especially Christmas gifts).
3. Initiate crafts within the family and make some of the needed gifts.
4. Draw family names for selected gifts rather than giving to everyone.

LIST OF DEBTS

TO WHOM OWED	CONTACT PHONE NO.	PAY OFF	PAYMENTS REMAINING	MONTHLY PAYMENT	DATE

IMPULSE LIST					
DATE	IMPULSE ITEM	1	2	3	

Figure 4.2

The Guideline Budget

THE GUIDELINE BUDGET

WHAT IS A GUIDELINE BUDGET?

A guideline budget is family spending divided into percentages to help determine the *proper balance* in each category of the budget, e.g., housing, food, and automobile.

The primary use of the guideline is to *indicate problem areas*. It is *not* an absolute. The percentages are based on a family of four people with incomes ranging from $15,000 to $60,000 per year. Above or below those limits, the percentages may change according to family situations and needs. In the lower income levels, basic family needs will dominate the income distribution.

PURPOSE OF A GUIDELINE

The guideline is developed to determine a standard against which to compare present spending patterns. It will serve as a basis for determining areas of overspending that are creating the greatest problems. Additionally, it helps to determine where adjustments need to be made. If you are overspending, the percentage guideline can be used as a goal for budgeting. Although the percentages are guides only, and *not* absolute, they do help to establish upper levels of spending.

For instance: A family spending 40 percent or more of their net spendable income on housing will have difficulty balancing their budget. There is little flexibility in most family incomes to absorb excessive spending on housing (or automobiles).

NET SPENDABLE INCOME

Review figure 5.1 and note that, once again, we start with gross income, less tithe and taxes, in order to determine the *net spendable income*. If taxes are known, then actual amounts can be used. For example, a family of four with an income of $18,000 per year would pay approximately 12 percent of gross income in taxes. For a single person making $12,000 a year, the tax burden will usually be 17 to 18 percent (based on the standard deduction).

GUIDELINE PERCENTAGES

The *net spendable income* is used to calculate the ideal spending for each budget category. In the example, net spendable income is $975 per month. Thus for housing, 32 percent of N.S.I. equals $312 per month. Therefore, about $312 and no more than $390 per month should be spent for housing, including payment, taxes, utilities, and upkeep.

Note that in some categories absolutes are impossible with variables such as utilities and taxes. You must adjust percentages within ranges under "Housing," "Food," and "Auto." Those three together cannot exceed 62 percent. Example: If 34 percent is used for housing, then 16 percent must be used for food and 12 percent for the auto.

The next step? Budget Analysis.

BUDGET PERCENTAGE GUIDELINES

Salary for Guideline = $15,000 /year

Gross Income Per month $1,250

Tithe	(10% of Gross)	(1250)	= $ 125
Tax	(12% of Gross)	(1250)	= $ 150
Net Spendable Income		975	
Housing	(32% of Net)	(975)	= $ 312 640
Food	(15% of Net)	(975)	= 146 300
Auto	(15% of Net)	(975)	= 146 300
Insurance	(5% of Net)	(975)	= 49
Debts	(5% of Net)	(975)	= 49 100
Entertain. & Rec.	(7% of Net)	(975)	= 68 140
Clothing	(5% of Net)	(975)	= 49 100
Savings	(5% of Net)	(975)	= 49 100
Medical	(5% of Net)	(975)	= 49 100
Miscellaneous	(6% of Net)	(975)	= 58 120
Total	(Cannot exceed Net Spendable Income)		$ 975

Figure 5.1

PERCENTAGE GUIDE FOR FAMILY INCOME

Gross Income	15,000	20,000	40,000	50,000	60,000
Tithe	10%	10%	10%	10%	10%
Taxes	12%	14%	15%	17%	21%
NET SPENDABLE	11,700	15,200	30,000	36,500	41,400
Housing	32%	30%	28%	25%	25%
Auto	15%	15%	12%	12%	12%
Food	15%	16%	14%	14%	10%
Insurance	5%	5%	5%	5%	5%
Entertainment/Rec.	7%	7%	7%	7%	7%
Clothing	5%	5%	5%	6%	6%
Medical/Dental	5%	5%	4%	4%	4%
Miscellaneous	6%	7%	7%	8%	8%
Savings	5%	5%	5%	5%	5%
Debts	5%	5%	5%	5%	5%
Investments	—	—	8%	9%	13%

Figure 5.2

SECTION 6
Budget Analysis

BUDGET ANALYSIS

After determining the present spending level (where you are), and reviewing the guideline percentages (where you should be), the task becomes one of developing a new budget that handles the areas of overspending. Keep in mind that the *total* expenditures must not exceed the net spendable income. If you have more spendable income than expenses, you need to control spending to maximize your surplus.

The Budget Analysis page (figure 6.1) provides space for summarizing both actual expenses and guideline expenses on one sheet for working convenience. The total amounts of each category from the Monthly Income and Expense sheet (figure 2.1) and from the Budget Percentage Guidelines (figure 5.1) should be transferred to the appropriate columns on the Budget Analysis page.

STEP ONE: COMPARE

The *Existing Budget* and *Guideline* columns should be compared. Note the difference, plus or minus, in the *Difference* column. A negative notation indicates a deficit; a positive notation indicates a surplus.

STEP TWO: ANALYZE

After comparing the *Existing* and *Guideline* columns, decisions must be made about overspending. It may be possible to reduce some areas to compensate for overspending in others. For example, if housing expenditures are more than 32 percent, it may be necessary to sacrifice in such areas as entertainment and recreation, miscellaneous, and automobiles. If debts exceed 5 percent, then the problems are compounded. Ultimately, the decision becomes one of where and how to cut back.

It is not necessary that your new budget fit the guideline budget. It is necessary that your new budget not exceed Net Spendable Income.

It is usually at this point that husband-wife communication is so important. No one person can make a budget work, because it may involve a family financial sacrifice. Without a willingness to sacrifice and establish discipline, no budget will succeed.

Note the flexibility gained if the family is not in debt. That 5 percent is available for use somewhere else in the budget.

STEP THREE: DECIDE

Once the total picture is reviewed, it is necessary to decide where adjustments must be made and spending reduced. It may be necessary to consider a change in housing, automobiles, insurance, private schools, etc.

The *minimum* objective of any budget should be to meet the family's needs without creating any further debt.

BUDGET ANALYSIS

Per Year ___15,000___ Net Spendable Income Per Month ___938___

Per Month ___1,250___

MONTHLY PAYMENT CATEGORY	EXISTING BUDGET	MONTHLY GUIDELINE BUDGET	DIFFERENCE + OR −	NEW MONTHLY BUDGET
1. Tithe	125	125	0	125
2. Taxes	187	150	+37	150
NET SPENDABLE INCOME (Per Month)	$ 938	$ 975	$ +37	$ 975
3. Housing	391	312	− 75	380
4. Food	230	146	− 84	200
5. Automobile(s)	85	146	+61	85
6. Insurance	39	49	+10	39
7. Debts	90	49	−41	75
8. Enter. & Recreation	53	68	+15	40
9. Clothing	50	49	−1	35
10. Savings	0	49	+49	40
11. Medical	30	49	+19	25
12. Miscellaneous	69	58	−11	56
TOTALS (Items 3 through 12)	$ 1037	$ 975	/////	$ 975

Figure 6.1

If there are debt problems, then begin by destroying all credit cards and other sources of credit. It may be necessary to negotiate with creditors to pay smaller amounts per month. It's better to establish an amount you can pay than to promise an amount you cannot.

Beware of consolidation loans, refinancing, and more borrowing. They are *not* the solutions; they are merely "symptom" treatments. The solution comes from discipline, sacrifice, and trusting God to supply needs.

After a new budget has been determined, you are ready to proceed to the allocation and control system.

How the adjustments were made:

Taxes:	Taxes were reduced because actual taxes with respect to gross income were less than withholding when all deductions were considered.
Housing:	There was an $11 reduction made. Hopefully, this can be saved by conserving on utilities. Although 40 percent is being spent for housing, it was decided not to move but rather to make sacrifices in the rest of the budget.
Food:	Note 15 percent used on the guideline. A target amount of $146 was set. Perhaps this can be improved upon with wise shopping.
Auto:	No change in this amount. Transportation will be adjusted to remain within the budget.
Insurance:	No change. A close evaluation of insurance needs and types of insurance may provide some savings here.
Debts:	A $15 reduction. Credit cards were cancelled. This shows commitment and paves the way for negotiations for lower payments.
Entertainment and Recreation:	A $40 target amount at least until debts are paid. Caution: Don't cut this out; cut it back.
Clothing:	Another cutback to make the budget fit.
Savings:	This was not in the existing spending. Get in the habit. It's the protection against future debt.
Medical:	A cut until debts are paid. Any unusual medical expenses after this will have to be covered by a rearrangement of the budget.
Miscellaneous:	A target amount. If it's not enough, then you will probably have to reduce entertainment and recreation or clothes.
Note:	The actual budget cannot exceed Net Spendable Income.

The Control System

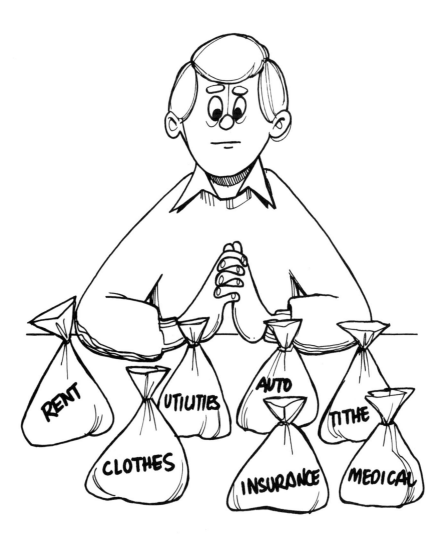

ACCOUNTING–ALLOCATION–CONTROL

A budget that is not used is a waste of time and effort. The most common reason a budget is discarded is because it's too complicated.

The system described in this workbook is the simplest, yet most complete possible.

KEEP IT SIMPLE

The Goal—Establish a level of spending for each category such that more money in does not mean more money to spend, and know where you are with respect to that level at all times.

This budget system is analogous to the old "envelope system." In the past, many employers paid earnings in cash. To control spending, families established an effective system by dividing the available money into the various budget categories (housing, food, clothes, etc.), then holding it in individual envelopes.

As a need or payment came due, money was withdrawn from the appropriate envelope and spent.

The system was simple and, when used properly, quite effective for controlling spending. The rule was simple: When an envelope was empty, there was no more spending for that category. Money could be taken from another envelope, but a decision had to be made—immediately.

Since most families today get paid by check, and since holding cash in the home is not always advisable, a different cash allocation system is necessary.

It is important to know how much *should* be spent and how much *is* being spent and how much is *left* to spend in each budget category. To accomplish this, account control pages have been substituted for envelopes. All the money is deposited into a checking account and account control pages are used to accomplish what the envelopes once accomplished. How much is put into each account (or envelope) from monies received during the month is determined from the Income Allocation sheet.

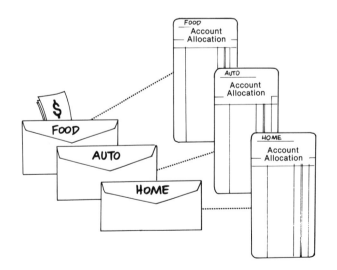

USE OF THE INCOME ALLOCATION PAGE (form 5)

The purpose of the income allocation page is to divide net spendable income among the various budget categories. It is simply a predetermined plan of how each paycheck or income source is going to be spent.

Once you have determined from the budget analysis how much can be spent in each category per month, write it in the *Monthly Allocation* column.

Next, divide the monthly allocation for each category (housing, food, etc.) by pay period.

EXAMPLE: Family income is received twice each month. Note that the mortgage
(Figure 8)   payment is made on the twenty-ninth of the month so the allocation must be divided in a manner to make sure that adequate funds are available at the time the payment is due. Utility and maintenance payments would have to be made from another pay period.

	ALLOCATION	PAY PERIOD	
HOUSING	$380	$170	$210
FOOD	$200	$100	$100
AUTO	$ 85	$ 42	$ 43
INSURANCE	$ 39	0	$ 39

It is not mandatory that checks be divided evenly. The important thing is that when a payment is due that the money be available. Therefore, some reserve funds from middle-of-the-month pay periods must be held to meet obligations that come due at the first of the month. Failure to do this is a common source of budget problems.

USE OF THE INDIVIDUAL ACCOUNT PAGES (form 7)
(Refer to figure 7.1)

A separate account page is used for each budget category (housing, food, auto, etc.) just as each had its own envelope under the cash system.

At the top of the page, the proper account title is entered (housing, food, etc.) together with the monthly allocation.

The purpose of the account sheet is to document ALL transactions for the month. The pay period allowance or allocation is shown as a deposit and, each time money is spent, it is shown as a withdrawal.

If funds are left at the end of the month, the account page is zeroed by transferring the money to the savings account. If an account runs short, then it may be necessary to transfer money from savings to the appropriate account. When an account is out of money a decision must be made concerning how it is going to be treated.

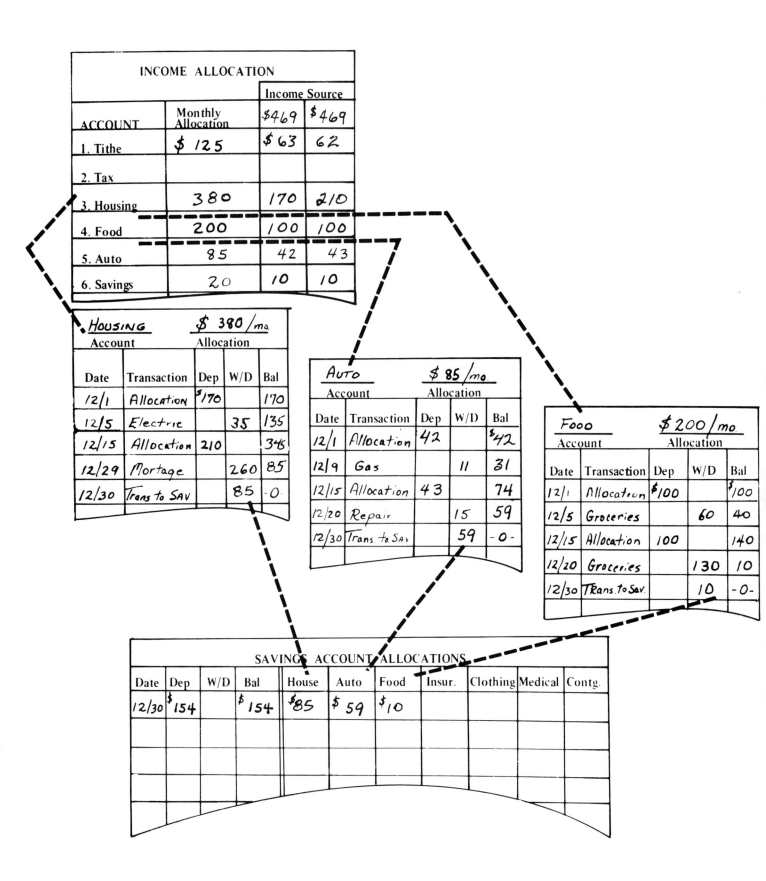

Figure 7.1

HOW TO USE THE SYSTEM

Figure 7.1 shows a typical family budget in which the take-home pay of $938 per month is received in two pay periods of $469 each.

PAY ALLOCATION—The two checks have been divided as evenly as possible among the necessary categories. For example, the tithe is paid each pay period (remember, it is based on gross income). The housing allocation of $380 is divided, $190 each pay period, and so on.

HOUSING ALLOCATION—On the first pay period, a deposit of $170 is noted on the account page. On the fifth, the electric bill is paid and noted as a withdrawal, leaving a balance of $135.

Each transaction is noted similarly until, at the end of the month, a balance of $85 is left. This balance is then transferred to savings, as are month-end balances from the other account pages (food, savings, etc.).

Hence, each account starts at zero the next month.

NOTE: In many cases, the housing account may have to carry a surplus forward to make the mortgage payment if it comes due on the first.

Keep in mind that the goal of the system is to establish a level of spending for each category and to know where you are with respect to that level.

The account pages ("envelopes") keep track of money in the checking account. The savings allocation page keeps track of money in the savings account. However, you may want to use a savings account page (or envelope) within the checking account to minimize transfers to and from the savings account.

Remember—the plan is to know what each dollar in the checking account is for and what each dollar in the savings account is for. When you spend money you need to know which money is spent (clothes money, food money, gas money, etc.).

DISCIPLINE

In order to provide the necessary control, you must discipline yourself to spend money based on the bottom line of the applicable envelope and not based on the bottom line of the checkbook.

PROBLEM AREAS

CASH WITHDRAWALS—Many times miscellaneous expenditures for car expenses, gas, etc. are made with personal cash. In establishing a budget, it is important to develop some rules for self-discipline.

1. Separate personal cash into categories indentical to the account pages. Use envelopes if necessary, but avoid spending gas money for lunches, and grocery money for entertainment.

2. When all the money has been spent from a category (entertainment, lunches, etc.) *stop spending.*

3. Don't write checks for amounts in excess of actual purchases to get cash. Write another check and note it as "cash, personal."

CATEGORY MIXING—Don't try to make the record-keeping more complicated than necessary. This system should require no more than thirty minutes per week to maintain. If you choose to develop more detailed breakdowns of expenses and savings, wait until the budget has been in use at least six months.

SECTION *8*

Begin Now

Scotland

$10 \text{ mos} \times 1000 = 10,000$

Christmas

MONTHLY INCOME & EXPENSES

INCOME PER MONTH	2724	**7.Debts**		
Salary – £	1458	Credit Card 475	125	
~~Interest~~ base J	546	Loans & Notes		
~~Dividends~~ T+C	720	Other ORU 450		80
Notes	___			
Rents	___	**8.Enter. & Recreation**	80	
		Eating Out		
TOTAL GROSS INCOME	2724	Trips		
		Babysitters		
LESS:		Activities		
1.Tithe	272	Vacation		
		Other		
2.Tax £318 $110	428	**9.Clothing**		50
NET SPENDABLE INCOME	2024	**10.Savings** – ORU 450 Scotland		
	205			35
3.Housing	5	**11.Medical Expenses**		
Mortgage (rent)	5	Doctor	10	
Insurance	89 (45)	Dentist 200	15	
Taxes		Drugs 10	10	
Electricity	35	Other		
Gas				80
Water	15	**12.Miscellaneous**		
Sanitation		Toiletry, cosmetics	20	
Telephone	50	Beauty, barber	10	
Maintenance	—	Laundry, cleaning	20	
Other		Allowances, lunches	—	
		Subscriptions	—	
4.Food	300	Gifts (incl. Christmas)	30	
	180	Special Education	—	
5.Automobile(s)		Cash		
Payments	—	Other		
Gas & Oil	150			
Insurance		**TOTAL EXPENSES**		930
License		– Debts ORU		– 450
Taxes		save		
Maint./Repair/ Replacement	30	**INCOME VS. EXPENSE**		
		Net Spendable Income		2024
6.Insurance	1			
Life		**Less Expenses**		1094
Medical				
Other				

48

FORM 1

MONTHLY INCOME & EXPENSES

INCOME PER MONTH	_____
Salary	_____
Interest	_____
Dividends	_____
Notes	_____
Rents	_____
TOTAL GROSS INCOME	_____
LESS:	
1. Tithe	_____
2. Tax	_____
NET SPENDABLE INCOME	_____
3. Housing	_____
Mortgage (rent)	_____
Insurance	_____
Taxes	_____
Electricity	_____
Gas	_____
Water	_____
Sanitation	_____
Telephone	_____
Maintenance	_____
Other	_____
4. Food	_____
5. Automobile(s)	_____
Payments	_____
Gas & Oil	_____
Insurance	_____
License	_____
Taxes	_____
Maint./Repair/ Replacement	_____
6. Insurance	_____
Life	_____
Medical	_____
Other	_____

7. Debts	_____
Credit Card	_____
Loans & Notes	_____
Other	_____
8. Enter. & Recreation	_____
Eating Out	_____
Trips	_____
Babysitters	_____
Activities	_____
Vacation	_____
Other	_____
9. Clothing	_____
10. Savings	_____
11. Medical Expenses	_____
Doctor	_____
Dentist	_____
Drugs	_____
Other	_____
12. Miscellaneous	_____
Toiletry, cosmetics	_____
Beauty, barber	_____
Laundry, cleaning	_____
Allowances, lunches	_____
Subscriptions	_____
Gifts (incl. Christmas)	_____
Special Education	_____
Cash	_____
Other	_____
TOTAL EXPENSES	_____
INCOME VS. EXPENSE	
Net Spendable Income	_____
Less Expenses	_____

FORM 1

VARIABLE EXPENSE PLANNING

Planning for those expenses that are not paid on a regular
monthly basis, by estimating the yearly cost and determining
the monthly amount needed to be set aside for that expense.
A helpful formula is to allow the previous year's expense and
add 5 percent.

	Estimated Cost	**Per Month**
1. VACATION	$_____ ÷ 12 =	$_____
2. DENTIST	$_____ ÷ 12 =	$_____
3. DOCTOR	$_____ ÷ 12 =	$_____
4. AUTOMOBILE	$_____ ÷ 12 =	$_____
5. ANNUAL INSURANCE	$_____ ÷ 12 =	$_____
(Life)	$_____ ÷ 12 =	$_____
(Health)	$_____ ÷ 12 =	$_____
(Auto)	$_____ ÷ 12 =	$_____
(Home)	$_____ ÷ 12 =	$_____
6. CLOTHING	$_____ ÷ 12 =	$_____
7. INVESTMENTS	$_____ ÷ 12 =	$_____
8. OTHER	$_____ ÷ 12 =	$_____
	$_____ ÷ 12 =	$_____

FORM 2

VARIABLE EXPENSE PLANNING

Planning for those expenses that are not paid on a regular monthly basis, by estimating the yearly cost and determining the monthly amount needed to be set aside for that expense. A helpful formula is to allow the previous year's expense and add 5 percent.

	Estimated Cost	Per Month
1. VACATION	$_____ ÷ 12 =	$_____
2. DENTIST	$_____ ÷ 12 =	$_____
3. DOCTOR	$_____ ÷ 12 =	$_____
4. AUTOMOBILE	$_____ ÷ 12 =	$_____
5. ANNUAL INSURANCE	$_____ ÷ 12 =	$_____
(Life)	$_____ ÷ 12 =	$_____
(Health)	$_____ ÷ 12 =	$_____
(Auto)	$_____ ÷ 12 =	$_____
(Home)	$_____ ÷ 12 =	$_____
6. CLOTHING	$_____ ÷ 12 =	$_____
7. INVESTMENTS	$_____ ÷ 12 =	$_____
8. OTHER	$_____ ÷ 12 =	$_____
	$_____ ÷ 12 =	$_____

FORM 2

BUDGET PERCENTAGE GUIDELINES

SALARY FOR GUIDELINE = _____/year

GROSS INCOME PER MONTH   _____

Tithe	(10% of Gross)	(_____)	= $_____
Tax	(12% of Gross)	(_____)	= $_____
NET SPENDABLE INCOME		(_____)	
Housing	(32% of Net)	(_____)	= $_____
Food	(15% of Net)	(_____)	= _____
Auto	(15% of Net)	(_____)	= _____
Insurance	(5% of Net)	(_____)	= _____
Debts	(5% of Net)	(_____)	= _____
Entertain. & Rec.	(7% of Net)	(_____)	= _____
Clothing	(5% of Net)	(_____)	= _____
Savings	(5% of Net)	(_____)	= _____
Medical/ Dental	(5% of Net)	(_____)	= _____
Miscellaneous	(6% of Net)	(_____)	= _____

TOTAL   (Cannot Exceed Net Spendable Income) $_____

FORM 3

BUDGET PERCENTAGE GUIDELINES

SALARY FOR GUIDELINE = _____/year

GROSS INCOME PER MONTH _____

Tithe	(10% of Gross)	(_____)	=	$_____
Tax	(12% of Gross)	(_____)	=	$_____
NET SPENDABLE INCOME		(_____)		
Housing	(32% of Net)	(_____)	=	$_____
Food	(15% of Net)	(_____)	=	_____
Auto	(15% of Net)	(_____)	=	_____
Insurance	(5% of Net)	(_____)	=	_____
Debts	(5% of Net)	(_____)	=	_____
Entertain. & Rec.	(7% of Net)	(_____)	=	_____
Clothing	(5% of Net)	(_____)	=	_____
Savings	(5% of Net)	(_____)	=	_____
Medical/ Dental	(5% of Net)	(_____)	=	_____
Miscellaneous	(6% of Net)	(_____)	=	_____

TOTAL (Cannot Exceed Net Spendable Income) $_____

FORM 3

BUDGET ANALYSIS

PER YEAR _____   NET SPENDABLE INCOME PER MONTH _____

PER MONTH _____

MONTHLY PAYMENT CATEGORY	EXISTING BUDGET	MONTHLY GUIDELINE BUDGET	DIFFERENCE + OR −	NEW MONTHLY BUDGET
1. Tithe				
2. Taxes				
NET SPENDABLE INCOME (PER MONTH)	$ _____	$ _____	$ _____	$ _____
3. Housing				
4. Food				
5. Automobile(s)				
6. Insurance				
7. Debts				
8. Enter. & Recreation				
9. Clothing				
10. Savings				
11. Medical				
12. Miscellaneous				
TOTALS (Items 3 through 12)	$ _____	$ _____	/////////	$ _____

FORM 4

BUDGET ANALYSIS

PER YEAR _____   NET SPENDABLE INCOME PER MONTH _____

PER MONTH _____

MONTHLY PAYMENT CATEGORY	EXISTING BUDGET	MONTHLY GUIDELINE BUDGET	DIFFERENCE + OR –	NEW MONTHLY BUDGET
1. Tithe				
2. Taxes				
NET SPENDABLE INCOME (PER MONTH)	$	$	$	$
3. Housing				
4. Food				
5. Automobile(s)				
6. Insurance				
7. Debts				
8. Enter. & Recreation				
9. Clothing				
10. Savings				
11. Medical				
12. Miscellaneous				
TOTALS (Items 3 through 12)	$	$	////	$

FORM 4

INCOME ALLOCATION

INCOME		INCOME SOURCE/PAY PERIOD			
BUDGET CATEGORY	**MONTHLY ALLOCATION**				
1. TITHE					
2. TAX					
3. HOUSING					
4. FOOD					
5. AUTO					
6. INSURANCE					
7. DEBTS					
8. ENTERTAINMENT & RECREATION					
9. CLOTHING					
10. SAVINGS					
11. MEDICAL/DENTAL					
12. MISCELLANEOUS					

FORM 5

INCOME ALLOCATION

INCOME		INCOME SOURCE/PAY PERIOD			
BUDGET CATEGORY	MONTHLY ALLOCATION				
1. TITHE					
2. TAX					
3. HOUSING					
4. FOOD					
5. AUTO					
6. INSURANCE					
7. DEBTS					
8. ENTERTAINMENT & RECREATION					
9. CLOTHING					
10. SAVINGS					
11. MEDICAL/DENTAL					
12. MISCELLANEOUS					

FORM 5

SAVINGS ACCOUNT ALLOCATIONS

Date	Deposit	With-draw	Balance	Housing	Food	Auto Insur.	Auto Maint.	Insur-ance	Clothes	Medical					

FORM 6

SAVINGS ACCOUNT ALLOCATIONS

Date	Deposit	With-draw	Balance	Housing	Food	Auto Insur.	Auto Maint.	Insur-ance	Clothes	Medical					

FORM 6

INDIVIDUAL ACCOUNT PAGE

ACCOUNT   ALLOCATION

DATE	TRANSACTION	DEPOSIT		W/DRAW		BALANCE	

FORM 7

INDIVIDUAL ACCOUNT PAGE

ACCOUNT   ALLOCATION

DATE	TRANSACTION	DEPOSIT		W/DRAW		BALANCE	

INDIVIDUAL ACCOUNT PAGE

ACCOUNT   ALLOCATION

DATE	TRANSACTION	DEPOSIT		W/DRAW		BALANCE	

INDIVIDUAL ACCOUNT PAGE

ACCOUNT   ALLOCATION

DATE	TRANSACTION	DEPOSIT		W/DRAW		BALANCE	

FORM 7

INDIVIDUAL ACCOUNT PAGE

ACCOUNT   ALLOCATION

DATE	TRANSACTION	DEPOSIT		W/DRAW		BALANCE	

INDIVIDUAL ACCOUNT PAGE

ACCOUNT   ALLOCATION

DATE	TRANSACTION	DEPOSIT		W/DRAW		BALANCE	

FORM 7

INDIVIDUAL ACCOUNT PAGE

ACCOUNT   ALLOCATION

DATE	TRANSACTION	DEPOSIT		W/DRAW		BALANCE	

INDIVIDUAL ACCOUNT PAGE

ACCOUNT   ALLOCATION

DATE	TRANSACTION	DEPOSIT		W/DRAW		BALANCE	

INDIVIDUAL ACCOUNT PAGE

ACCOUNT _____   ALLOCATION _____

DATE	TRANSACTION	DEPOSIT	W/DRAW	BALANCE

INDIVIDUAL ACCOUNT PAGE

ACCOUNT   ALLOCATION

DATE	TRANSACTION	DEPOSIT		W/DRAW		BALANCE	

INDIVIDUAL ACCOUNT PAGE

ACCOUNT _____   ALLOCATION _____

DATE	TRANSACTION	DEPOSIT	W/DRAW	BALANCE

FORM 7

INDIVIDUAL ACCOUNT PAGE

ACCOUNT   ALLOCATION

DATE	TRANSACTION	DEPOSIT		W/DRAW		BALANCE	

FORM 7

INDIVIDUAL ACCOUNT PAGE

ACCOUNT   ALLOCATION

DATE	TRANSACTION	DEPOSIT		W/DRAW		BALANCE	

FORM 7

INDIVIDUAL ACCOUNT PAGE

ACCOUNT _____   ALLOCATION _____

DATE	TRANSACTION	DEPOSIT		W/DRAW		BALANCE	

FORM 7

INDIVIDUAL ACCOUNT PAGE

ACCOUNT   ALLOCATION

DATE	TRANSACTION	DEPOSIT		W/DRAW		BALANCE	

FORM 7

INDIVIDUAL ACCOUNT PAGE

_____   _____
ACCOUNT   ALLOCATION

DATE	TRANSACTION	DEPOSIT		W/DRAW		BALANCE	

FORM 7

LIST OF DEBTS

TO WHOM OWED	CONTACT NAME PHONE NO.	PAY OFF	PAYMENTS LEFT	MONTHLY PAYMENT	DATE

FORM 8

LIST OF DEBTS

TO WHOM OWED	CONTACT NAME PHONE NO.	PAY OFF	PAYMENTS LEFT	MONTHLY PAYMENT	DATE

FORM 8

ADDENDUM
DETERMINING INSURANCE NEEDS

HOW MUCH INSURANCE DO I NEED?

HOW MUCH INSURANCE CAN I AFFORD?

The amount of life insurance a family needs depends on many variables such as family income, ages of the children, ability of the wife to earn an income, Social Security status, the standard of living you hope to provide, and outstanding debts.

Form 9 will assist in determining what the requirements are. The requirements will then have to be weighed against the budget. If the budget dollars are limited, it will be necessary to get as much insurance as possible for the available dollar.

See the Insurance Needs Worksheet (form 9).

PRESENT INCOME PER YEAR

How much income is being provided by the breadwinner of the family? The goal is to provide for the family so that they may continue the same living standard they enjoy under this income.

PAYMENTS NO LONGER REQUIRED

Family expenses should drop as a result of the death of the breadwinner. For example: a second car may no longer be required; less income (or different income) will mean less taxes; activities or hobbies would not be an expense; investments or savings may be reduced or stopped.

INCOME AVAILABLE

The breadwinner's death may initiate income from some other sources. Social Security income will depend on one's eligibility which, in turn, is determined by the time in the system, amount of earnings and ages of spouse and dependent children. Income may also be available from retirement plans, investments, annuities, etc.

The income-earning potential of the wife is a definite asset to the family. Ages of the children are a factor here. A minimum insurance program should provide time for obtaining or sharpening job skills if necessary.

ADDITIONAL INCOME REQUIRED TO SUPPORT FAMILY

The income presently being earned, less the payments no longer required, and less the income available, results in the income that needs to be supplied in order for the family to continue living on the same level enjoyed through the income of the husband.

INSURANCE REQUIRED TO PROVIDE THE NEEDED INCOME

If provision could be made in an "ideal" manner, the insurance money invested at 10 percent would return the needed amount of income to the family. To find the required amount of insurance, multiply the income required to support the family by 10.

> EXAMPLE: $7,000 additional income is required to support the family; $7,000 x 10 = $70,000. $70,000 in insurance invested at 10 percent would provide the needed funds.

LUMP SUM REQUIREMENTS

In addition to the insurance required to produce the regular sustained income, lump sums may be required for specific purposes (e.g., college education). Those needs should be determined and added to the total amount of insurance.

Are funds needed to pay off the home mortgage? This should be discussed as a part of the family plan. If mortgage payments are being made under the existing income, then this could be continued under the sustained income provision. Since paying for the home would significantly boost the insurance requirement, this will also raise the amount that must be spent for insurance.

ASSETS AVAILABLE

Determine the assets that are available for family provision. Subtract this amount from the desired amount of insurance.

Equity in a home can be counted as an asset only if the survivors plan to sell it.

TOTAL INSURANCE NEEDED

The total tells how much insurance is needed. This must be balanced against how much can be spent for insurance. If the insurance dollars are limited, it will be necessary to get as close to the plan as possible with those dollars. Term insurance with its lower initial premiums probably offers the best opportunity for adequate provision with fewest dollars.

The plan should also include instructions as to how the insurance money is to be used.

NOTE:

Insurance needs should be reviewed periodically. Family changes (i.e., new additions, children becoming employed or leaving home, inflation changes, income changes, etc.) should prompt an insurance review.

INSURANCE NEEDS WORKSHEET

PRESENT INCOME PER YEAR

_____
Line 1

PAYMENTS NO LONGER REQUIRED
    Estimated Living Cost (for Husband)   _____
    Life Insurance   _____
    Savings   _____
    Investments   _____
    Taxes   _____

    _____   _____

    _____   _____

    Total =   _____
Line 2

INCOME REQUIRED TO SUPPORT FAMILY

(Line 1 - Line 2) = _____
Line 3

INCOME AVAILABLE
    Social Security   _____
    Wife's Income   _____
    Retirement Plans   _____
    Investments   _____

    _____   _____

    _____   _____

    Total =   _____
Line 4

ADDITIONAL INCOME REQUIRED TO SUPPORT FAMILY

(Line 3 - Line 4) = _____
Line 5

INSURANCE REQUIRED TO PROVIDE THE NEEDED INCOME

(Line 5 x 10 = _____ x 10) = _____
Line 6

LUMP SUM REQUIREMENTS
    Debt Payments   _____
    Funeral Costs   _____
    Estate Tax & Settlement Costs   _____
    Education Costs   _____

    _____   _____

    _____   _____

    Total =   _____
Line 7

TOTAL FUNDS REQUIRED

(Line 6 + Line 7) = _____
Line 8

ASSETS AVAILABLE
    Real Estate   _____
    Stocks and Bonds   _____
    Savings   _____

    _____   _____

    _____   _____

    Total =   _____
Line 9

TOTAL INSURANCE NEEDED   (Line 8 - Line 9) = _____

FORM 9

INSURANCE NEEDS WORKSHEET

PRESENT INCOME PER YEAR _____
Line 1

PAYMENTS NO LONGER REQUIRED
Estimated Living Cost (for Husband) _____
Life Insurance _____
Savings _____
Investments _____
Taxes _____
_____ _____
_____ _____

Total = _____
Line 2

INCOME REQUIRED TO SUPPORT FAMILY

(Line 1 - Line 2) = _____
Line 3

INCOME AVAILABLE
Social Security _____
Wife's Income _____
Retirement Plans _____
Investments _____
_____ _____
_____ _____

Total = _____
Line 4

ADDITIONAL INCOME REQUIRED TO SUPPORT FAMILY

(Line 3 - Line 4) = _____
Line 5

INSURANCE REQUIRED TO PROVIDE THE NEEDED INCOME

(Line 5 x 10 = _____ x 10) = _____
Line 6

LUMP SUM REQUIREMENTS
Debt Payments _____
Funeral Costs _____
Estate Tax & Settlement Costs _____
Education Costs _____
_____ _____
_____ _____

Total = _____
Line 7

TOTAL FUNDS REQUIRED (Line 6 + Line 7) = _____
Line 8

ASSETS AVAILABLE
Real Estate _____
Stocks and Bonds _____
Savings _____
_____ _____
_____ _____

Total = _____
Line 9

TOTAL INSURANCE NEEDED (Line 8 - Line 9) = _____

FORM 9